HOW-TO LIBRARY

FOLDING ORIGAMI

By Dana Meachen Rau • Illustrated by Kathleen Petelinsek

CHERRY LAKE PUBLISHING • ANN ARBOR, MICHIGAN

CHERRY
LAKE
Publishing

Published in the United States of America
by Cherry Lake Publishing
Ann Arbor, Michigan
www.cherrylakepublishing.com

Content Adviser: Dr. Julia L. Hovanec, Professor of Art Education,
Kutztown University, Kutztown, Pennsylvania

Photo Credits: Page 4, ©arsentev/Shutterstock, Inc.; page 5, ©Kotomiti
Okuma/Shutterstock, Inc.

Library of Congress Cataloging-in-Publication Data
Rau, Dana Meachen, 1971–
  Folding origami / by Dana Meachen Rau.
     pages cm. — (How-to library) (Crafts)
  Audience: Grade 4 to 6.
  Includes bibliographical references and index.
  ISBN 978-1-62431-145-1 (library binding) — ISBN 978-1-62431-
277-9 (paperback) — ISBN 978-1-62431-211-3 (e-book) 1. Origami—
Juvenile literature. I. Title.

  TT872.5.R38 2013
  736'.982—dc23   2013014983

Cherry Lake Publishing would like to acknowledge the work
of The Partnership for 21st Century Skills. Please visit
www.p21.org for more information.

Printed in the United States of America
Corporate Graphics, Inc.
July 2013
CLFA13

A NOTE TO ADULTS: Please review the instructions for these craft projects before your children make them. Be sure to help them with any steps you do not think they can safely do on their own.

A NOTE TO KIDS: Be sure to ask an adult for help with these craft activities when you need it. Always put your safety first!

HOW-TO LIBRARY

TABLE OF CONTENTS

Sculpting with Paper…4

Basic Tools…6

Folds and Creases…8

Origami Symbols…10

Building from Bases…12

Making Origami Paper…14

Book of Great Ideas…16

Rainbow Wheel…18

Robot Nesting Boxes…20

Yawning Cats…22

Fruit Bowl…24

Flapping Bird…26

Share Your Creations…29

Glossary…30
For More Information…31
Index…32
About the Author…32

Sculpting with Paper

You can fold paper into almost any shape you can imagine.

You can create a **three-dimensional** sculpture with just a small, flat square of paper. That may seem hard to believe, but it's true! Origami is the art of paper folding. The word *origami* comes from the Japanese words *ori*, which means "to fold," and *kami*, which means "paper."

Origami has a long history. Folded paper creations were used for special occasions in Japan hundreds of years ago. For example, butterflies were exchanged by the bride and groom at wedding ceremonies. Many **traditional** Japanese origami designs were passed down through families. In the mid-1800s in Europe, Friedrich Frobel invented the idea of kindergarten. Kindergarten teachers started using origami to educate young children.

Origami as we know it today began in the mid-1900s when expert paper folder Akira Yoshizawa began publishing books of origami designs. He created a system of symbols to help people understand origami instructions. This helped transform origami from a craft activity into an art form.

Most of the models in this book are based on traditional Japanese designs. Give these projects a try. Then let your own imagination fly! How will you sculpt your ideas in paper?

Some origami designs are shaped like animals.

Basic Tools

You only need two things to make an origami creation—
a piece of paper and your hands!

Paper

Origami paper is thin and colored or decorated on one side.
The other side is usually white. It comes in various sizes. The
larger the paper, the larger your model will be. If you are
trying origami for the first time, you might want to start large.
You can work your way down to smaller sizes.

You don't have to use origami paper for your projects. You
can use any paper that holds **creases** well. Many craft stores
sell scrapbooking paper, which comes in many colors and
designs. You can use pages from magazines, wrapping
paper, decorated napkins, or even a dollar bill. Card
stock is a thick paper. It is not as easy to fold,
but is good to use when your model needs to
be more **durable**.

Other Tools

Other tools can help you fold and decorate
your project:

Bone folder: Some artists use
this to help make sharp creases.

You can use your thumbnail just as well. But a bone folder can be helpful with thick paper, such as card stock.

Scissors and ruler: If you want to cut your paper smaller, you will need a ruler for measuring and a good pair of paper scissors for cutting. You can also use a paper cutter for a more **precise** cut.

Needle and thread: A needle and thread will help you hang your creations from a ceiling or mobile.

Glue, tape, markers, crayons, stickers, paint, etc.: These tools can be used to hold together or decorate your origami creations.

FROM A RECTANGLE TO A SQUARE

Most origami creations are made from a single piece of square paper. You can make a quick square out of a rectangular piece of paper without measuring. Fold the top right corner down toward the bottom edge. Carefully line the edges up, and crease the folded edge. Cut off the strip of extra paper on the side. Now you have a square!

Folds and Creases

An origami creation is simply a series of folds and creases. There are a few different kinds of folds that you will use to make the projects in this book.

Crease

In some projects you will need to crease the paper. That means you fold it, press down along the edge, and unfold it again. This leaves a line for you to use as a reference for other folds.

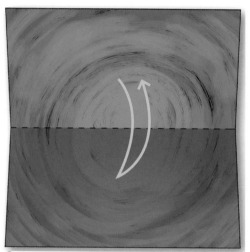

Crease

Pinch Crease

Start to fold the paper but don't press down along the entire edge. Just crease the ends. Then unfold the paper. This gives you a small reference point instead of a whole line.

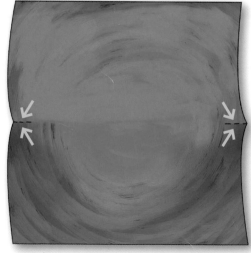

Pinch

Valley Fold

Fold the paper toward you so that it makes a V, or valley shape. It is shown in directions with a dashed line.

Mountain Fold

Fold the paper away from you, so that it makes a pointed mountain shape. It is shown in directions with a dotted and dashed line.

Squash Fold

Open the flaps of a folded piece of paper. Line up the top corner to the bottom edge. Then squash the paper flat, creasing it along the new triangle edges.

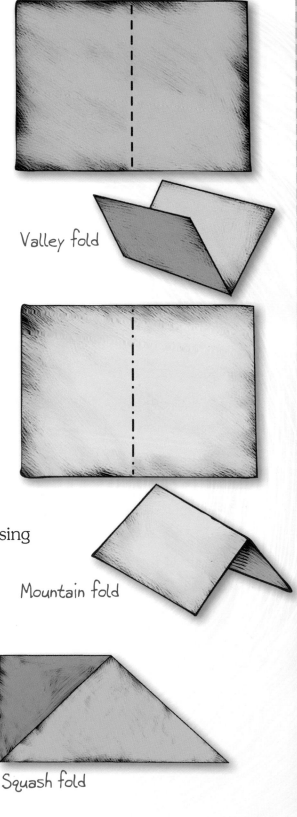

Valley fold

Mountain fold

Squash fold

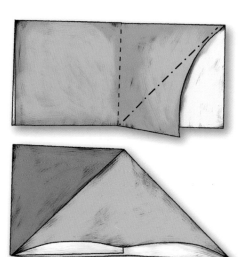

9

Origami Symbols

Origami instructions are easy to follow if you know the language. Arrows, lines, and dots are used to show which folds you need to make. See the chart on the opposite page.

Tips

- Try to make your creases and folds as sharp as possible. Press down your folds with your finger in the middle first, and then run your thumbnail along the edge to each end. You can also use a bone folder to make a sharper fold or crease.
- Always fold on a flat surface. Your folds and creases won't be sharp or even if you try to fold your project in your hands.
- Look at each instruction carefully. In most steps, you will make a square, rectangle, or triangle shape out of the paper. Notice when you have to line up these shapes along creases, or how tall or wide they need to be. Also notice when to flip the project over.
- If you are confused by an instruction, look ahead to the next step to see how it should look next. That may help you figure out what to do.

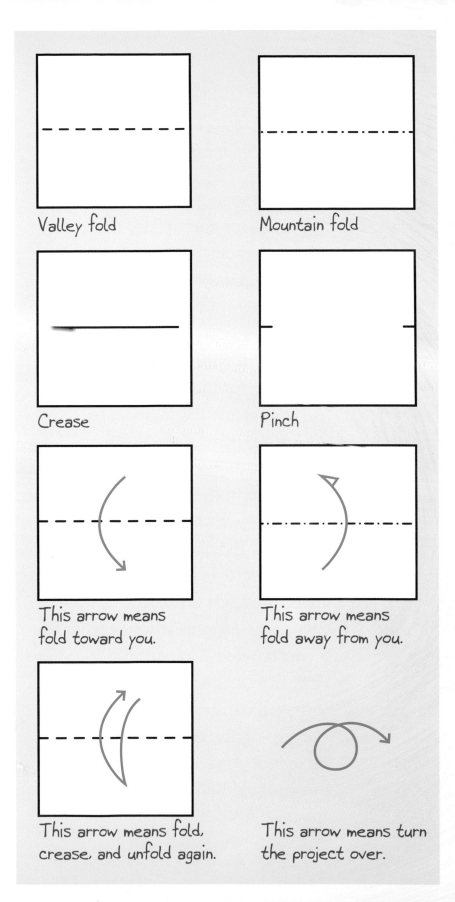

Valley fold

Mountain fold

Crease

Pinch

This arrow means fold toward you.

This arrow means fold away from you.

This arrow means fold, crease, and unfold again.

This arrow means turn the project over.

Building from Bases

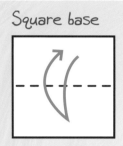

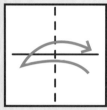

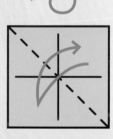

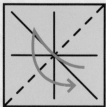

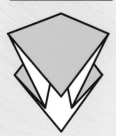

Below are base shapes that are used for many origami projects. They are good practice for reading origami instructions and symbols. Try them out before you tackle a larger project.

Square Base Steps

Use this base for the rainbow wheel (*see pages 18–19*) and the flapping bird (*see pages 26–28*).

1. With the white side of the paper up, valley fold in half from top to bottom. Crease. Unfold.
2. Valley fold in half from side to side. Crease. Unfold. Turn the project over so the colored side is up.
3. Valley fold diagonally from corner to corner. Crease. Unfold.
4. Valley fold diagonally from the other corner to corner. Crease. Unfold.
5. Push up on the center of the paper to make it pop up. Bring the opposite corners together. Press the paper flat so you have a square shape.

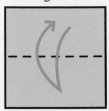
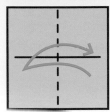

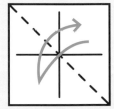
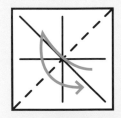

Triangle Base Steps

Use this base for the fruit bowl (*see pages 24–25*).

1. With the colored side of the paper up, valley fold in half from top to bottom. Crease. Unfold.
2. Valley fold in half from side to side. Crease. Unfold. Turn the project over so the white side is up.
3. Valley fold diagonally from corner to corner. Crease. Unfold.
4. Valley fold diagonally from the other corner to corner. Crease. Unfold.
5. Turn the paper over so the colored side is up. Push up on the center of the paper to make it pop up. Bring the center of opposite edges together. Press flat so you have a triangle shape.

Blintz Base Steps

Use this base for the robot nesting boxes (*see pages 20–21*) and the yawning cats (*see pages 22–23*).

1. With the white side of the paper facing up, valley fold in half from top to bottom. Crease. Unfold.
2. Valley fold in half from side to side. Crease. Unfold.
3. Valley fold each corner into the center.

Blintz base

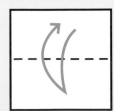
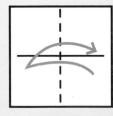
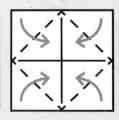

Making Origami Paper

Make your own patterned paper!

You can buy interesting origami paper at a store, but you can also make your own unique patterns!

Cover your workspace with newspaper. Cover yourself with a smock or apron. Lay out your supplies. You will need a few pieces of white copy paper, acrylic water-based paint, brushes, a container of water, a paper plate to use as a **palette**, and paper towels. Now its time to play with paint!

Squeeze a few colors of paint onto your palette. Dip your brush in the water and then in the paint. Now cover your paper in a fun design! Play around with different strokes—straight, wavy, and diagonal. The paint should be thin. If it is too thick, the paint may crack when you try to fold the paper. Try combining colors and making patterns. Let the papers dry when you are done painting.

Here are some ideas for adding details to your designs:

- Cardboard Combs: Cut out a small piece of cardboard. Then cut slits along one side. Bend up every other slit to make a comb. Paint a layer of paint onto your paper, and then swipe the comb over the surface. Try crisscrossing the lines to make interesting patterns.

- Speckling: Dip an old toothbrush into paint. Hold the toothbrush over the paper, and then run your finger along the bristles. It will speckle the paint onto the paper.

- Sponges and Stamps: Dip a sponge into paint, and then dab it all over the surface of your paper. You can also use a ready-made stamp and ink pad to add decorative shapes.

- Markers: Draw doodles, dots, and squiggles! There is no limit to the designs you can create. When the papers are dry, cut them into squares for your origami projects.

Book of Great Ideas

Make a minibook using simple mountain and valley folds. Fill it with your ideas and sketches for future origami projects!

Materials

- 3 8½ x 11-inch (22 x 28 cm) pieces of white copy paper
- 1 8½ x 11-inch (22 x 28 cm) piece of card stock paper (any color)

Steps

1. Start with a piece of white paper. Pinch crease to find the center. Then valley fold the bottom and top edges to the center pinch crease.
2. Valley fold the paper in half from side to side. Then mountain fold each side to the center. Now you have a zigzag of mountain and valley folds. Repeat steps 1 and 2 with another piece of white paper.
3. Repeat step 1 with the third piece of white paper. But this time, flip the project over. Valley fold the middle, and mountain fold the sides as described in step 2.

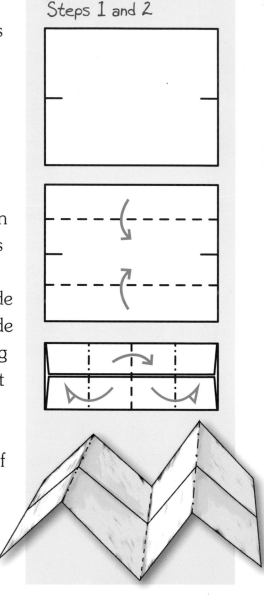

Steps 1 and 2

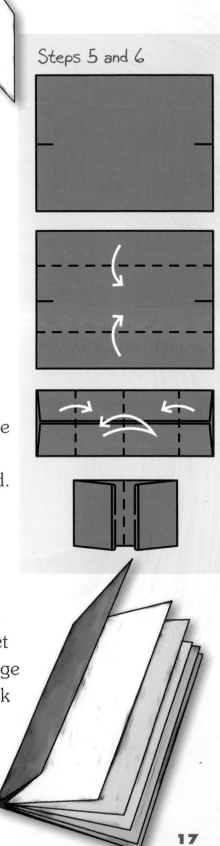

4. Slide the end of one paper into the end of the next. Repeat this until you have created one continuous accordion strip of paper. The flat sides should be in front and the seam sides should be in back.

5. To make a cover, pinch crease the colored card stock paper. Valley fold the bottom and top to about ¼ inch (0.5 cm) from the center pinch crease. There should be space between the edges.

6. Valley fold the paper in half. Unfold. Valley fold the two sides to about ¼ inch (0.5 cm) from the center crease, again leaving a small space between them.

7. Slide the first "page" of your accordion strip into the front pocket of the cover piece. Slide the last page of your accordion strip into the back pocket of the cover piece.

8. Tuck the accordion pages in, and close the cover like a book.

Rainbow Wheel

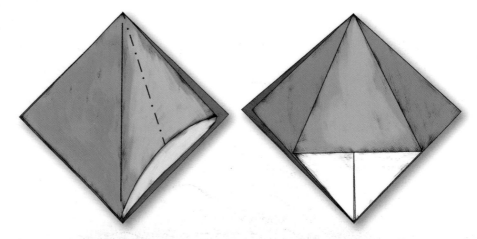

When you make a bunch of
origami pieces and fit them
together into a design, it is called **modular** origami.
Use rainbow colors to create a three-dimensional piece to
dress up the top of a present. The bow will be part of the gift!

Materials
- 8 4½-inch (11 cm) squares of
  origami paper, in rainbow colors
- White glue

Steps
1. Fold a square base (*see page 12*).
2. Squash fold the right flap to the center crease (*see page 9*).
   Now your piece has two flaps on one side and one flap on
   the other.

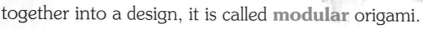

3. Repeat steps 1 and 2 with the remaining seven pieces of paper.
4. To fit your pieces together into a wheel shape, insert the flap of one piece in between the two flaps of another piece. Use a little glue to hold them together.
5. Continue until all the pieces are connected.
6. Tape this colorful decoration to the top of a gift!

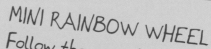

MINI RAINBOW WHEEL
Follow the same instructions as above, but use smaller, $1\frac{1}{2}$-inch (4 cm) square papers. You can glue this minidecoration on a card to go with your gift, or you can make a card to mail. The design can easily be flattened to fit inside an envelope.

Robot Nesting Boxes

This project uses a design called the *masu* box. A masu box is a wooden box traditionally used for measuring rice in Japan. Make a bunch of boxes in different sizes. Nest them inside one another and cover them with a lid. No one will expect all of the surprises inside!

Materials

Square pieces of card stock in gray, silver, or black in the following sizes:

- 12 inches (30 cm, for the lid)
- 11½ inches (29 cm, for the largest box)
- 10½ inches (27 cm)
- 9 inches (23 cm)
- 7½ inches (19 cm)
- 6 inches (15 cm)
- 4½ inches (11 cm, for the smallest box)
- Small scraps of paper and glue for decoration

Steps

1. Start with a blintz base (*see page 13*).
2. Valley fold the sides into the center. Crease and unfold.
3. Unfold two triangle flaps on opposite sides.
4. Valley fold the folded sides into the center.
5. Lift the folded sides slightly. Then lift the top pointed end and bring it toward the center. At the same time, tuck in the edges and fold them on their creases to form the sides of the box. Fold the pointed end down into the box.
6. Repeat step 5 on the other side. If the paper does not sit flat on the bottom, secure it with a small dab of glue.
7. Repeat steps 1 through 6 with all of the other papers so that you have seven boxes of various sizes. The largest box is the cover.
8. Decorate your boxes with robot details or some other design of your choice.

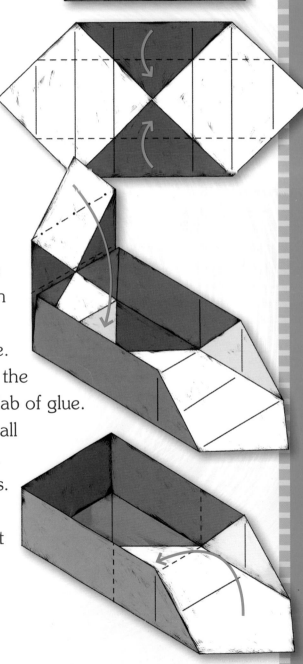

Yawning Cats

This cat hand puppet is worn-out from all the folding! She can't stop yawning. Use a smaller piece of paper to make her a kitten.

Materials

- 6-inch (15 cm) square orange origami paper (or any cat color)
- 3½-inch (9 cm) square origami paper of a matching color

Steps

1. Start with a blintz base (*see page 13*). Turn it over.
2. Valley fold each corner into the center.

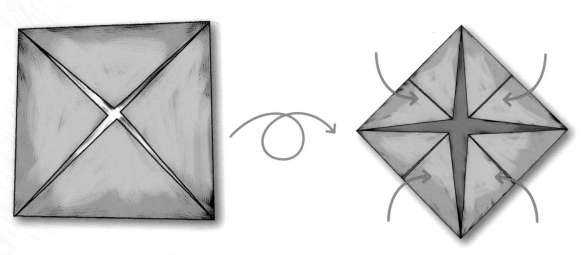

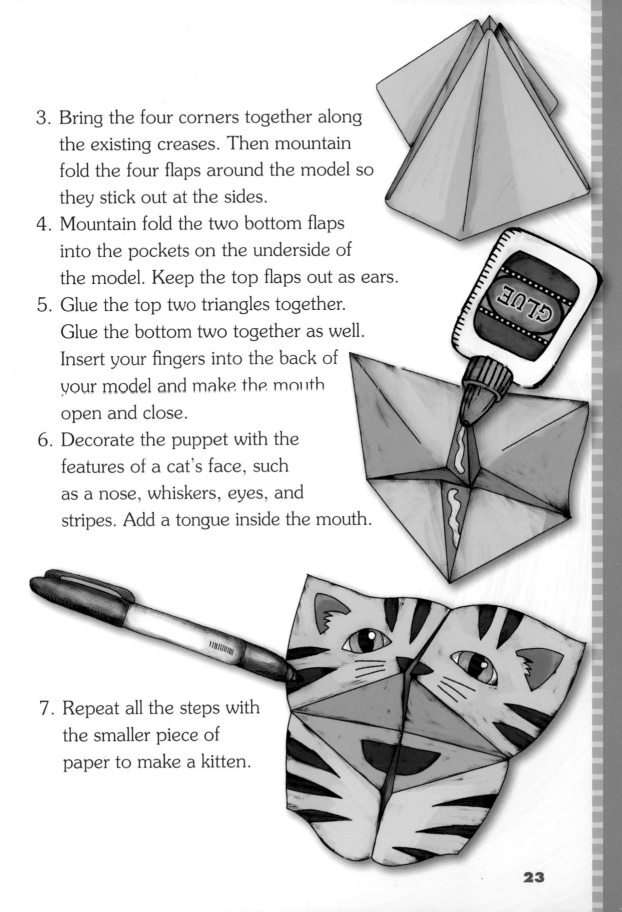

3. Bring the four corners together along the existing creases. Then mountain fold the four flaps around the model so they stick out at the sides.

4. Mountain fold the two bottom flaps into the pockets on the underside of the model. Keep the top flaps out as ears.

5. Glue the top two triangles together. Glue the bottom two together as well. Insert your fingers into the back of your model and make the mouth open and close.

6. Decorate the puppet with the features of a cat's face, such as a nose, whiskers, eyes, and stripes. Add a tongue inside the mouth.

7. Repeat all the steps with the smaller piece of paper to make a kitten.

Fruit Bowl

This traditional origami model is called the water bomb. You can use it to make a bowl of fruit. Use larger papers for apples and oranges. Use smaller papers for grapes or berries. Display your creations in a bowl!

Materials

- 1 6-inch (15 cm) square red origami paper (for an apple)
- 1 6-inch (15 cm) square green origami paper (for an apple)
- 1 6-inch (15 cm) square orange origami paper (for an orange)
- 1 6-inch (15 cm) square purple origami paper (for a plum)
- 3 3-inch (8 cm) square blue origami papers (for blueberries)
- Toothpick (if needed)
- 4-inch (10 cm) square brown origami papers (for stems)
- Green origami paper (for leaves)
- White glue

Steps

1. Start with a triangle base (*see page 13*).
2. Valley fold the corners of the top layer up to the top point.
3. Valley fold the corners of the top layer into the center.

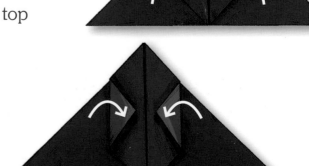

4. Valley fold the top tips down.
5. Tuck these flaps into the pockets so that they lie flat.
6. Turn the piece over. Repeat steps 1 to 5 on this side.
7. Hold two opposite flaps in your fingers, and find the end with the small hole. Blow into the hole to **inflate** the cube with air. If it doesn't fully inflate, you can stick a toothpick in the hole and use it to help push out the sides.
8. Cut the brown origami paper in half. Roll up each half starting from the short ends. These will be your stems. Stick the stems in the top of the fruits.
9. Cut out leaf details from a piece of green origami paper. Glue them on the top of the fruits to make leaves. Repeat steps 1-9 to make a second apple, a plum, an orange, and three blueberries.

Blow here to inflate

Flapping Bird

Birds are a very common origami shape. This design is tricky, so take your time. After you've made one bird, keep practicing your origami skills and make a whole flock!

Materials

- 1 6-inch (15 cm) square origami paper (any color)
- Pencil

Steps

1. Start with a square base (*see page 12*).
2. Valley fold both sides of the top layer to the center to make a kite shape. Unfold.
3. Valley fold the top point down. Crease. Unfold.
4. Turn the model over. Repeat steps 2 and 3.

5. Unfold the side flaps. Lift the bottom point upward. Mountain fold the side creases. Press flat.

6. Turn the project over. Repeat step 5 on the other side.

7. Open the right flap, and then press it down toward the left. Turn the project over and repeat on the other side.

8. Valley fold the bottom point to the top points. Turn over and repeat on the other side.

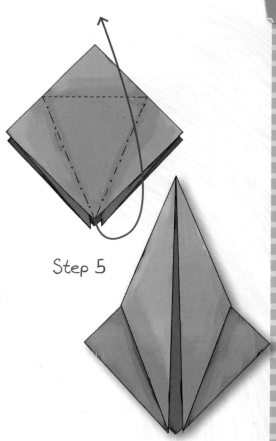

Step 5

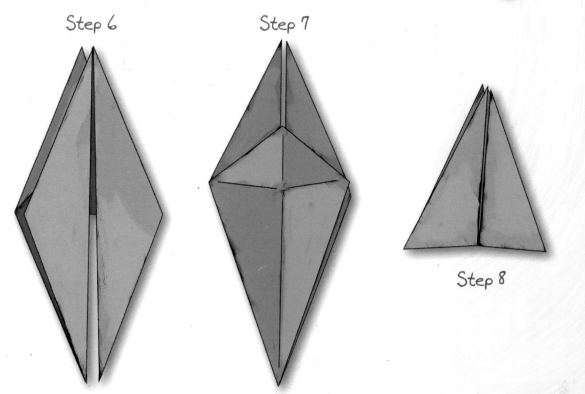

Step 6

Step 7

Step 8

9. Gently pull out the points on the right and left (these will be the head and tail). On the bottom of the model, press the new creases flat so the points stick out the sides.

10. To make the head, bend the tip downward, mountain fold the sides, and valley fold the center. Press the new creases.

11. Roll each wing around a pencil so that it curves outward.

HOW TO MAKE THE BIRD FLAP

Hold your model at the bottom point on the head side with your thumb and forefinger. With your other hand, pull the tail up and down. The bird's wings will flap!

Share Your Creations

How will you share your paper creations?

You can make them into ornaments by using a needle and thread. Poke a small hole in the top or center of the piece and pull the thread through. Knot the ends. Hang your creation on a tree branch or make lots of designs to make a mobile.

At a party, you can scatter origami models on a table as place cards or party favors. Use huge pieces of paper to fold larger decorations to hang from the ceiling.

Write a note to a friend, and then fold it up into a bird, cat, or piece of fruit! Your friend can unfold your gift to get the message.

Or just make origami for yourself. Take the time to pause in your busy day. Carry on the tradition of folding paper to make amazing creations.

PRACTICE MAKES (ALMOST) PERFECT

Your first attempts at origami may come out lopsided. The sides may not be symmetrical. But keep practicing! The more you try the better you'll get. Don't get frustrated if your creation isn't perfect. Crafts are often more special when you can tell they are homemade.

Glossary

creases (KREE-siz) folds or lines in fabric or paper

durable (DOOR-uh-buhl) tough and lasting for a long time

inflate (in-FLAYT) to make something expand by blowing or pumping air into it

modular (MAJ-uh-lur) made up of several different pieces of similar size

palette (PAL-uht) a flat board that is used for mixing paints

precise (pri-SISE) very accurate or exact

symmetrical (suh-MET-ri-kuhl) having matching parts or shapes on both sides of a dividing line

three-dimensional (THREE duh-MEN-shuhn-uhl) having the three dimensions of length, width, and height

traditional (truh-DISH–uhn-uhl) having to do with customs, ideas, or beliefs that are handed down from one generation to the next

For More Information

Books

Boursin, Didier. *Origami for Everyone: Beginner, Intermediate, Advanced*. Buffalo, NY: Firefly Books, 2011.

Catel, Patrick. *Japan*. Chicago: Heinemann Library, 2012.

Jackson, Paul, and Miri Golan. *Origami Zoo: 25 Fun Paper Animal Creations*. Layton, UT: Gibbs Smith, 2011.

Meinking, Mary, and Chris Alexander. *Easy Origami: A Step-By-Step Guide for Kids*. Mankato, MN: Capstone Press, 2010.

Nguyen, Duy. *Monster Origami*. New York: Sterling, 2007.

Web Sites

Exploratorium Magazine: Exploring Paper

www.exploratorium.edu/exploring/paper

To learn more about the ancient art of origami.

Origami USA

http://origamiusa.org

Check out this site for origami tips and sample projects to try.

Index

blintz base, 13
bone folders, 6–7, 10
book of great ideas project, 16–17

cardboard combs, 15
crayons, 7
creases, 6–7, 8, 10, 11

details, 15

flapping bird project, 12, 26–28
folds, 10, 11
fruit bowl project, 13, 24–25

glue, 7

history, 4–5

markers, 7, 15
masu boxes, 20
mini rainbow wheel project, 19
modular origami, 18

mountain folds, 9, 11

needles, 7

ornaments, 29

paint, 7, 14, 15
paper, 6, 7, 14–15, 19
paper cutters, 7
pinch creases, 8, 11

rainbow wheel project, 12, 18–19
robot nesting boxes project, 13, 20–21
rulers, 7

scissors, 7
sharing, 29
speckling, 15
sponges, 15
square base, 12
square paper, 7, 19
squash folds, 9
stamps, 15

stickers, 7
symbols, 5, 10–11
symmetry, 29

tape, 7
thread, 7, 29
traditions, 4–5
triangle base, 13

valley folds, 9, 11

word origin, 4

yawning cats project, 13, 22–23
Yoshizawa, Akira, 5

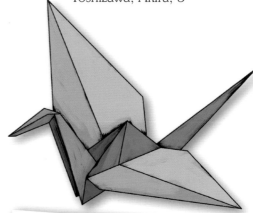

About the Author

Dana Meachen Rau is the author of more than 300 books for children on many topics, including science, history, cooking, and crafts. She creates, experiments, researches, and writes from her home office in Burlington, Connecticut.